Spotlight On

Civic Courage

Heroes of Conscience™

Rosa Parks

Civil Rights Activist

Avery Elizabeth Hurt

Rosen YA™

New York

Published in 2018 by The Rosen Publishing Group, Inc.
29 East 21st Street, New York, NY 10010

First Edition

Library of Congress Cataloging-in-Publication Data

Names: Hurt, Avery Elizabeth, author.
Title: Rosa Parks : civil rights activist / Avery Elizabeth Hurt.
Description: New York, NY : Rosen Publishing Group, Inc., 2018. | Series: Spotlight on civic courage: heroes of conscience | Includes bibliographical references and index. | Audience: Grades 5–10.
Identifiers: LCCN 2017013021| ISBN 9781538381052 (library bound) | ISBN 9781538381021 (pbk.) | ISBN 9781538381069 (6 pack)
Subjects: LCSH: Parks, Rosa, 1913–2005—Juvenile literature. | African Americans—Alabama—Montgomery—Biography—Juvenile literature. | African American women—Alabama—Montgomery—Biography—Juvenile literature. | Civil rights workers—Alabama—Montgomery—Biography—Juvenile literature. | African Americans—Civil rights—Alabama—Montgomery—History—20th century—Juvenile literature. | Segregation in transportation—Alabama—Montgomery—History—20th century—Juvenile literature. | Montgomery (Ala.)—Race relations—Juvenile literature.
Classification: LCC F334.M753 P3743 2017 | DDC 323.092 [B]—dc23
LC record available at https://lccn.loc.gov/2017013021

Manufactured in the United States of America

On the cover: This Rosa Parks photo is dated June 14, 1999. Her refusal to change her seat in 1955 spurred the Montgomery bus boycott, shown in the background photo dated 1956.

CONTENTS

"No"

It had been a long day, and Rosa Parks may have been tired. She boarded the Cleveland Avenue bus that would take her home from work, and took a seat just behind the "whites only" section of the bus. Soon the front of the bus, where only white people were allowed to sit, filled up. A white man boarded the bus, and the driver told Parks to give the man her seat. Parks didn't move. The bus driver shouted at her to give up her seat. Parks said, simply, "No."

The driver told her that if she didn't get up, he would have her arrested. She answered calmly, "You may do that."

The bus driver did have her arrested. And that was the beginning of the Montgomery bus boycott and the start of the civil rights movement.

Later Rosa Parks said she *was* tired—tired of giving in to white people.

In an act that took a great deal of courage, Rosa Parks refused to give up her seat on the bus to a white person.

Jim Crow

In 1896, the US Supreme Court ruled that it was legal to have separate facilities for black and white Americans. This meant that black people could be forced not only to sit in the backs of buses so that white people could sit up front but they also had to go to separate schools, drink from separate water fountains, and eat in separate restaurants. The system of laws and customs that enforced these and many other differences was called Jim Crow (after a common derogatory nickname for blacks), and it was very much in place in 1955, when Rosa Parks refused to give up her seat.

Having to go to a different school or ride in a separate part of the bus may not seem like a big deal. But making black people use separate facilities showed that white people thought blacks were so inferior they could not even sit beside them.

An African American man enters a movie theater in Belzoni, Mississippi, by the back entrance, obeying the customs of Jim Crow.

A scuffle breaks out when two black students are ordered off the sidewalk in segregated Little Rock, Arkansas, during the Jim Crow years.

Jim Crow was not only a system of laws but also a system of etiquette. Blacks were expected to treat whites with deference. Black people had to use the terms "Mr." and "Miss" or "ma'am" and "sir" when speaking to whites, but white people never used these titles of respect for blacks. Whites called blacks by their first names or simply called black males "boy"—even if the black person was a grown man. It was a completely humiliating experience for black people.

It was also dangerous. Blacks who violated Jim Crow laws—or even Jim Crow etiquette—could lose their homes or their jobs or even be killed. Because whites ran the court systems, white people were rarely punished for crimes against blacks.

When Rosa Parks refused to give up her seat, she was taking a brave stand. It was not the first nor would it be the last time Parks was brave.

Dangerous to Be Black

Rosa Parks was born Rosa Louise McCauley on February 4, 1913, in Tuskegee, Alabama. When Rosa was still a young child, her parents separated and she and her mother moved to Pine Level, Alabama, to live with her mother's parents, who had been born slaves. Rosa's grandfather, Sylvester Edwards, had a permanent limp from being beaten by white overseers. When she was an adult, Rosa wrote, "In my lifetime I have known Negroes who were killed by whites, without any arrests or investigations … It is the custom to keep such things covered up." The Ku Klux Klan (KKK), a group that intimidates

blacks (as well as Jews, immigrants, and homosexuals) and works to deny them their civil rights, was very active when Rosa was a child. The KKK often went on "night rides" near Rosa's home, burning black churches and schools and killing and beating black people.

Racial violence was not limited to the southern United States. In this photo, the KKK is parading in London, England, in 1951.

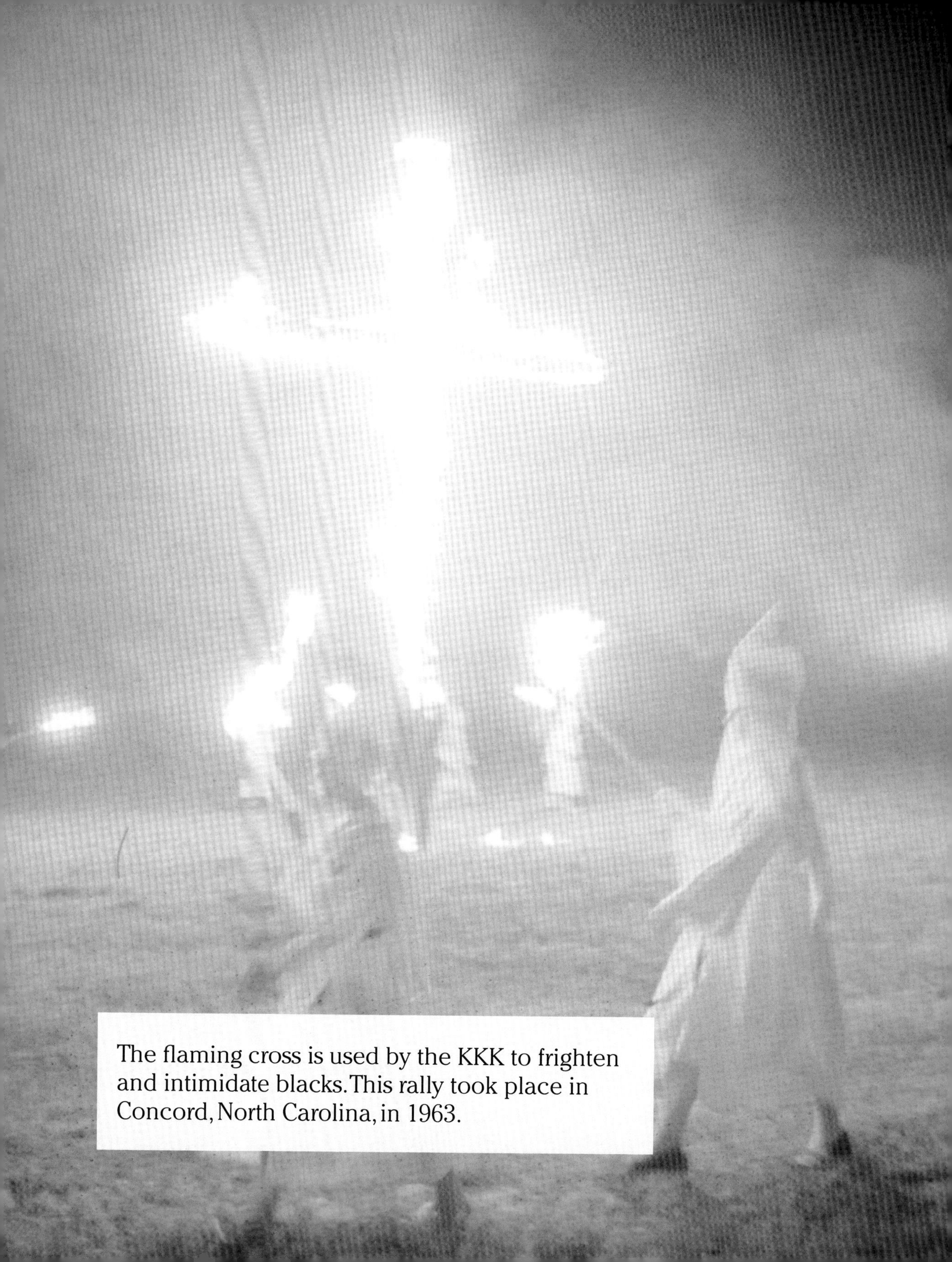

The flaming cross is used by the KKK to frighten and intimidate blacks. This rally took place in Concord, North Carolina, in 1963.

The windows and doors of Rosa's grandparents' home were nailed shut from the inside and boarded up at night. When she was a little girl, Rosa often joined her grandfather as he sat in the living room at night with a shotgun on his lap, protecting his family from marauding Klan members. Rosa often went to bed with her clothes on so that she would be ready to run if she had to. Of course, Rosa was frightened of the Klan members with their white hoods and burning torches, but she was also incredibly brave. She learned from her grandfather that it was important to protect others as well as oneself. Simply being a black person in that time and place was dangerous, and achieving anything meant taking risks. Rosa would quickly learn how to make those risks count—not just for herself but for others in her community.

Dignity and Self-Respect

When Rosa was eleven, her mother, a teacher who valued education, sent her to live with relatives in Montgomery so she could attend the Montgomery Industrial School for Girls, a school dedicated to educating black girls as well as giving them a sense of pride and self-esteem. The school had been started in 1886 by Alice White and Margaret Beard, two white women from Massachusetts. The girls learned vocational skills—sewing, cooking, and basic health care—as well as academic subjects like reading, writing, and math. But the most important thing Rosa learned at Miss White's school

was, as she wrote in her autobiography, “that I was a person with dignity and self-respect, and I should not set my sights lower than anybody else just because I was black. We were taught to be ambitious and to believe that we could do what we wanted in life.”

Parks used the sewing skills she learned at Miss White’s school in her job as a seamstress in a Montgomery department store.

No Pushing

Even though Rosa was a gentle, somewhat shy child, she was never a pushover. In fact, someone tried pushing her over once—quite literally—and it didn't go well. One day, while Rosa was walking to school, a white boy on roller skates tried to push her off the sidewalk while she was walking home from school. Rosa pushed him back. The boy's mother threatened to have Rosa arrested. Rosa calmly explained that the boy had pushed her first and pointed out that she "wasn't bothering him at all." She didn't end up in jail this time, but Rosa's mother did move her to stay with relatives who lived in another part of town so that Rosa didn't have to walk through a white neighborhood on her way to school. It was clear even then that Rosa was not going to accept unfair treatment without standing up for herself.

Rosa Parks was a dignified, gentle woman—but she was never timid or fainthearted. All her life she was willing to take risks for what was right.

Birth of an Activist

Rosa Parks's childhood had prepared her for speaking up and fighting back against injustice, but it wasn't until she met her future husband that she found a way to make a real difference. Raymond Parks was a barber in Montgomery when he and Rosa married in 1932. He was the first real activist Rosa had ever met. He was a member of the National Association for the Advancement of Colored People (NAACP), and he was secretly helping raise money to pay the legal fees of the Scottsboro Boys, nine young African American teenagers who had been falsely accused of raping a white woman

and were facing the death penalty. The police had killed several people who were involved with the effort to help the Scottsboro Boys. Rosa was impressed by Raymond's courage and commitment, and soon she became an activist, too.

Parks helped save the lives of these nine boys—the Scottsboro Boys—who were falsely accused of raping a white woman and condemned to death. They were not exonerated until 2013.

A Glimpse of a Better World

In 1941, Parks had begun working at Maxwell Field, which is now Maxwell Air Force Base, in Montgomery. That same year, President Franklin Roosevelt had signed Executive Order 8802, which forbade racial discrimination in the military. When Parks rode the trolley on base to her work site, white people and black people sat together wherever they could find a seat. Parks often sat with a white woman and her little boy, and they would talk during their ride. This was the first time Parks had experienced a world where black people and white people were treated the same. It was a nice way to live. She learned that Roosevelt had signed the order only after civil rights leaders—especially A. Philip Randolph, an African American labor leader—threatened to organize a march on Washington if he didn't. Parks saw that political activism had the power to change the world.

Labor leader A. Philip Randolph, a longtime activist for social and economic justice, was a primary force behind the desegregation of the US defense industry.

Not Too Timid

Raymond Parks thought it was too dangerous for his wife to join the NAACP, but when Rosa learned that a former female classmate was a member of the Montgomery branch, she also joined the organization, in December 1943. Rosa Parks was soon asked to be secretary, and as she put it in her memoirs, she was "too timed to say no." She was not, however, too timid to get involved in the civil rights work the group was doing. Parks wrote letters, sent press releases to newspapers, and kept records of discrimination and acts of violence against black people. She gathered evidence that would help bring charges against white people who harmed or murdered black people. Though Parks and the NAACP didn't have much success in those early years, they did, as she put it, "let it be known that we did not wish to continue being treated as a second-class citizen."

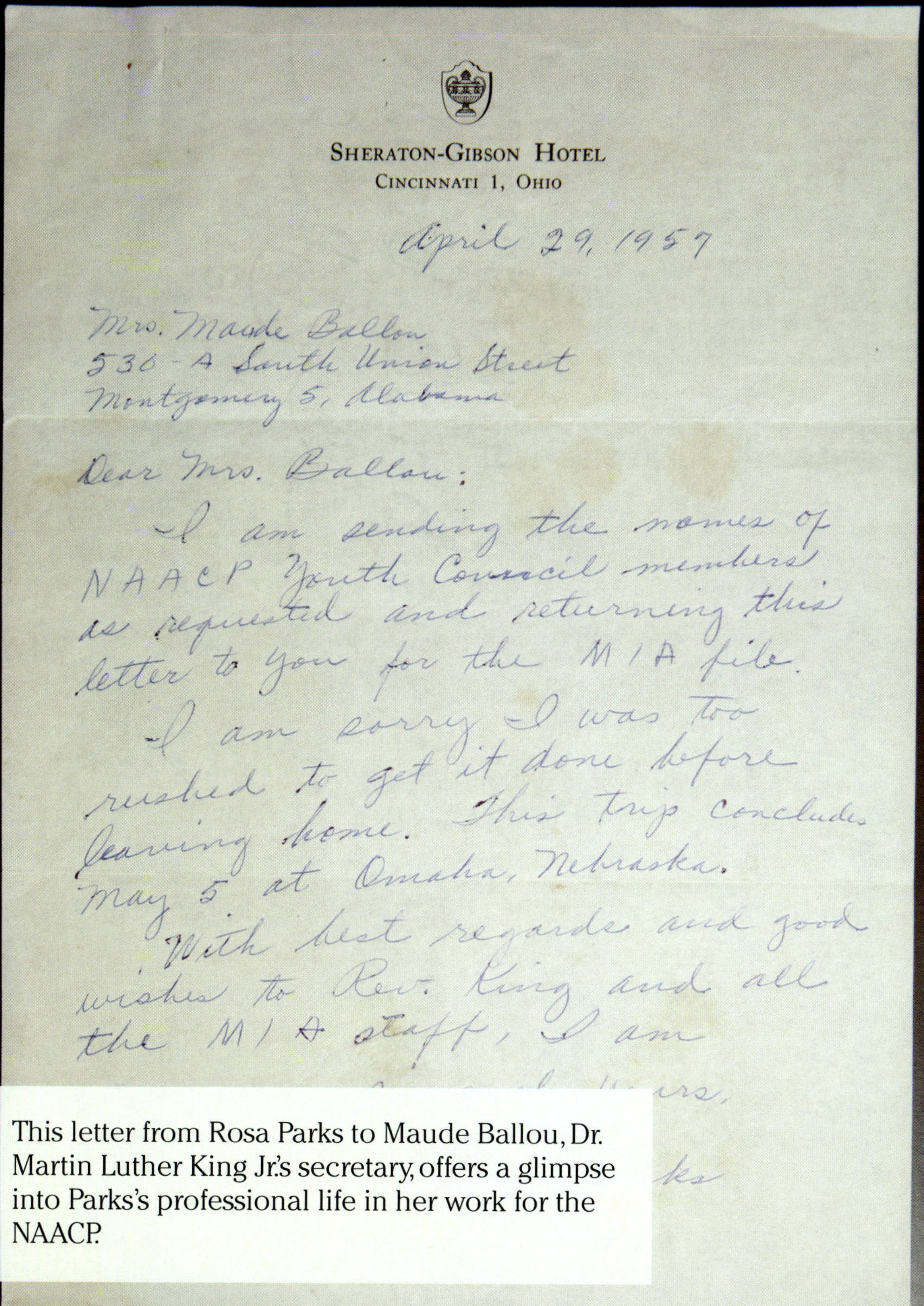

SHERATON-GIBSON HOTEL
CINCINNATI 1, OHIO

April 29, 1957

Mrs. Maude Ballou
530-A South Union Street
Montgomery 5, Alabama

Dear Mrs. Ballou:

I am sending the names of NAACP Youth Council members as requested and returning this letter to you for the MIA file.

I am sorry I was too rushed to get it done before leaving home. This trip concludes May 5 at Omaha, Nebraska.

With best regards and good wishes to Rev. King and all the MIA staff, I am

This letter from Rosa Parks to Maude Ballou, Dr. Martin Luther King Jr.'s secretary, offers a glimpse into Parks's professional life in her work for the NAACP.

Trying to Vote

In 1870, the Fifteenth Amendment gave African American men the right to vote, and in 1920 all women got the right to vote. But in practice it was difficult for blacks to exercise that right. Some states passed laws allowing only people who owned property to vote. People were often required to pay a tax before they could vote. These measures were just disguised ways to prevent blacks from voting.

When Parks tried to register to vote, she had to take a test. She knew the correct answers, but was told she didn't pass. The next time she tried to register, she made a copy of her answers so she could bring a lawsuit against the state of Alabama if the registrar said she didn't pass. That time she was given a voting certificate. For blacks, simply exercising their constitutional rights took courage and a willingness to fight.

Black men got the right to vote fifty years before women of any color did. But in practice, blacks were, more often than not, prevented from exercising that right.

Enough Is Enough

By the time Parks took a seat on the Cleveland Avenue bus on December 1, 1955, she had fought many quiet battles against injustice. Once before she had been forced off a bus for not boarding the bus at the back. Nor was Parks the first black person to refuse to give up her seat for a white person. Just that spring, a teenage girl named Claudette Colvin had been arrested for refusing to give up her seat, and Parks had helped raise money for Colvin's legal defense. Until now, though, blacks hadn't demanded an end to segregation, only that they be treated with a little more respect on the buses. But this time, when Parks went to jail rather than give in to white privilege, she started a movement that would change the world. Parks wasn't the only one who was tired of giving in to white people.

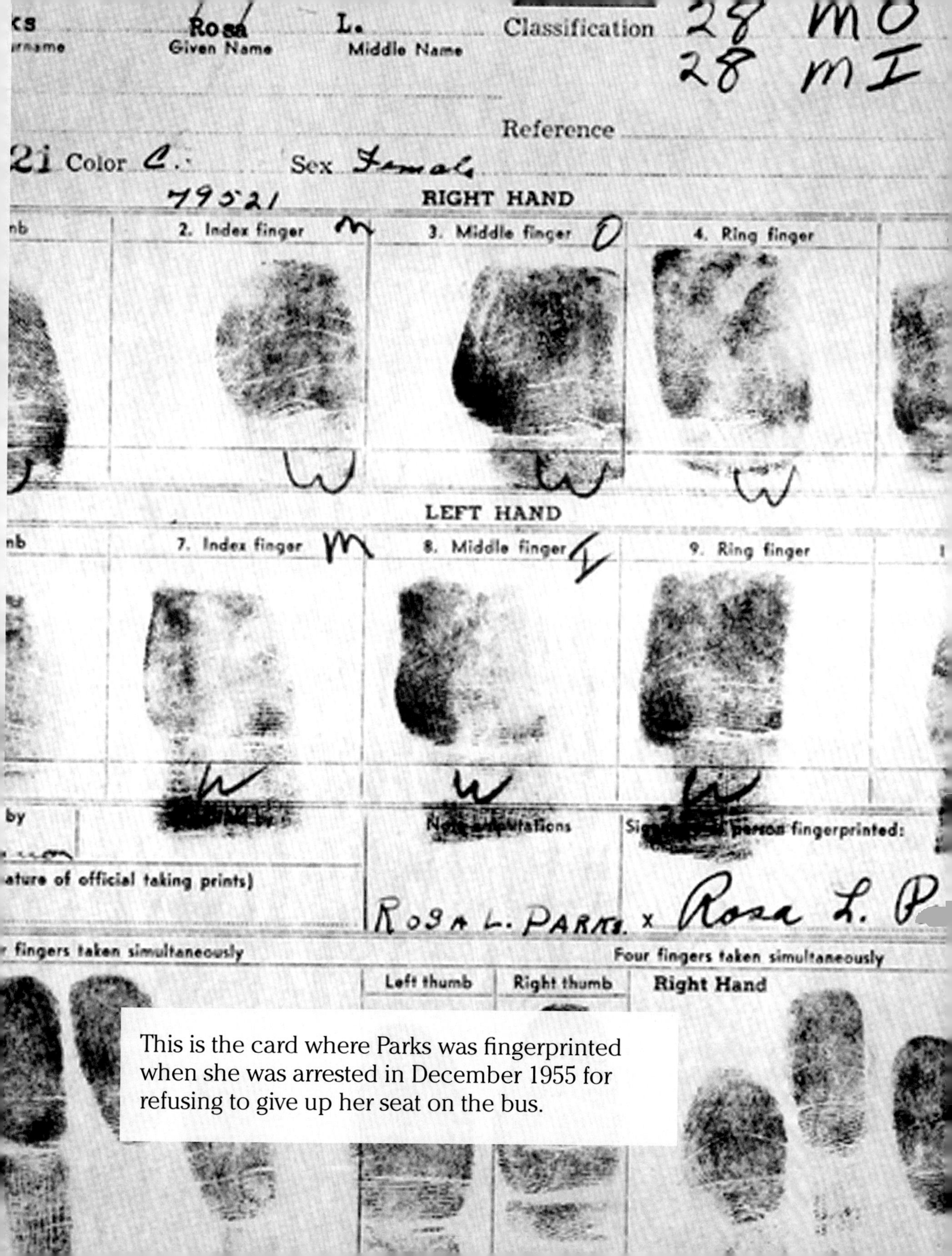

This is the card where Parks was fingerprinted when she was arrested in December 1955 for refusing to give up her seat on the bus.

Boycott

The very night Parks was arrested, the black community began organizing. The local chapter of the NAACP made flyers calling for a citywide bus boycott to protest Parks's arrest and distributed them in black schools and churches. The following Monday morning, December 5, the day of Parks's trial, empty buses rolled through the streets of Montgomery as thousands of African Americans walked to their jobs rather than taking the buses. "Never before had the black community of Montgomery united in protest," Parks later wrote. And that was just the beginning. Activists realized that they could use the momentum of the successful bus boycott to build a bigger crusade. They formed the Montgomery Improvement Association (MIA) and elected as its leader Dr. Martin Luther King Jr., the new pastor of the Dexter Avenue Baptist Church. Parks's arrest and the boycott it sparked were the beginning of the civil rights movement.

The Reverend Martin Luther King Jr. in his vestments as minister of the Dexter Avenue Baptist Church in Montgomery, Alabama, where he would help organize the bus boycott

Resistance

Organizers had intended for the bus boycott to last only that one day. However, African Americans continued to avoid the buses—costing the city of Montgomery a lot of revenue. Of course, it was very hard on the protesters, too. The MIA organized volunteer drivers and black churches raised money to buy station wagons to take people to work. Even some sympathetic whites contributed. Parks volunteered as a dispatcher taking calls from people who needed rides. The city responded with threats and intimidation. Police officers arrested carpool drivers for the slightest traffic violations. They sent threatening letters to white people who gave rides to

the protesters. Parks received telephone calls from people saying she should be killed. Dr. King's home and the home of the president of the Montgomery NAACP were bombed. No one was injured in those blasts, but it was clear that the fight was not going to be easily won.

Dr. King, Rosa Parks, Ralph Abernathy, and other civil rights leaders meet to discuss strategies for the Montgomery bus boycott.

Victory

While the black citizens of Montgomery were keeping up the boycott, the movement's lawyers and leaders had been working through the court system to challenge Montgomery's bus segregation laws. On November 13, 1956, the US District Court ruled in *Browder v. Gayle* that bus segregation was unconstitutional. As soon as the official, written order arrived from the court, on December 20, 1956, the boycott ended, 381 days after it began.

This was not the end of the movement. It was just the beginning. The efforts of Rosa Parks and the other leaders of the Montgomery bus boycott proved that peaceful, organized protest and hard work both in the

courts and in the streets—even in the face of intense and often violent resistance—could bring about change and help achieve racial justice. But it was not easy, and there were hard times ahead for the civil rights movement and for Rosa Parks.

Rosa Parks and other African Americans peacefully board a Montgomery bus, along with white riders, after the successful conclusion of the Montgomery bus boycott.

A New Home

After the bus boycott, Rosa Parks and her husband had difficulty finding jobs in Montgomery. So in 1957, Parks, her husband, and her mother moved to Detroit, Michigan. Raymond Parks worked as an instructor at a barber college, and she remained active in the civil rights movement, speaking at meetings and attending marches around the country.

In 1964, President Lyndon Johnson signed the Civil Rights Act, national legislation that ended segregation and discrimination based on race, color, religion, sex, or national origin. In 1965, he signed the Voting Rights Act, which gave the federal government the right to oversee elections in states with a history of denying citizens their right to vote. These laws did not solve all the problems of African Americans, but they did provide legal means of challenging injustices. Parks's fight was not over, but the work she had been doing since she was a young woman was finally getting results.

The US civil rights movement inspired people worldwide. Parks's Detroit house was rescued from demolition and relocated to Berlin, Germany, as a monument to Parks and her civil rights legacy.

Continuing the Fight

For the rest of her life, Parks fought injustice wherever she found it. As an assistant to US congressman John Conyers of Michigan (for whom she worked for twenty years), she helped find housing for homeless people. She continued to speak and march for civil rights and women's rights. Parks did not limit her political activism to the United States; in the 1980s she spoke out against apartheid in South Africa. When she was seventy-four years old, she founded the Rosa and Raymond Parks Institute for Self-Development, an organization dedicated to helping struggling young people reach their highest potential. In the last few years of her life, she spoke out against the military response to the 9/11 attacks. She began her life of activism working quietly with the Montgomery NAACP and ended it as one of the most respected and inspiring political activists of the twentieth century.

Parks waits in Statuary Hall in the US Capitol before being presented with the Congressional Gold Medal for service to her country.

THE NATION PAYS ITS RESPECTS

Rosa Parks died on October 24, 2005, at age ninety-two. Her body lay in state in the Capitol Rotunda. She was the first woman and the second African American to be honored in this way. Forty thousand Americans came to pay their respects, including the first African American secretary of state, Condoleezza Rice. Rice said, "Without Mrs. Parks, I probably would not be standing here today as secretary of state."

At Parks's funeral, people remembered her as a soft-spoken, quiet woman, and indeed she was. But clearly, Rosa Parks did not live a quiet life. She was a brave freedom fighter and political activist who risked her life to, as President George W. Bush put it,

“hold our nation true to the words of its founding document.” Rosa Parks proved that in order to be brave, you do not have to be aggressive, and persistence in the face of resistance can change the world.

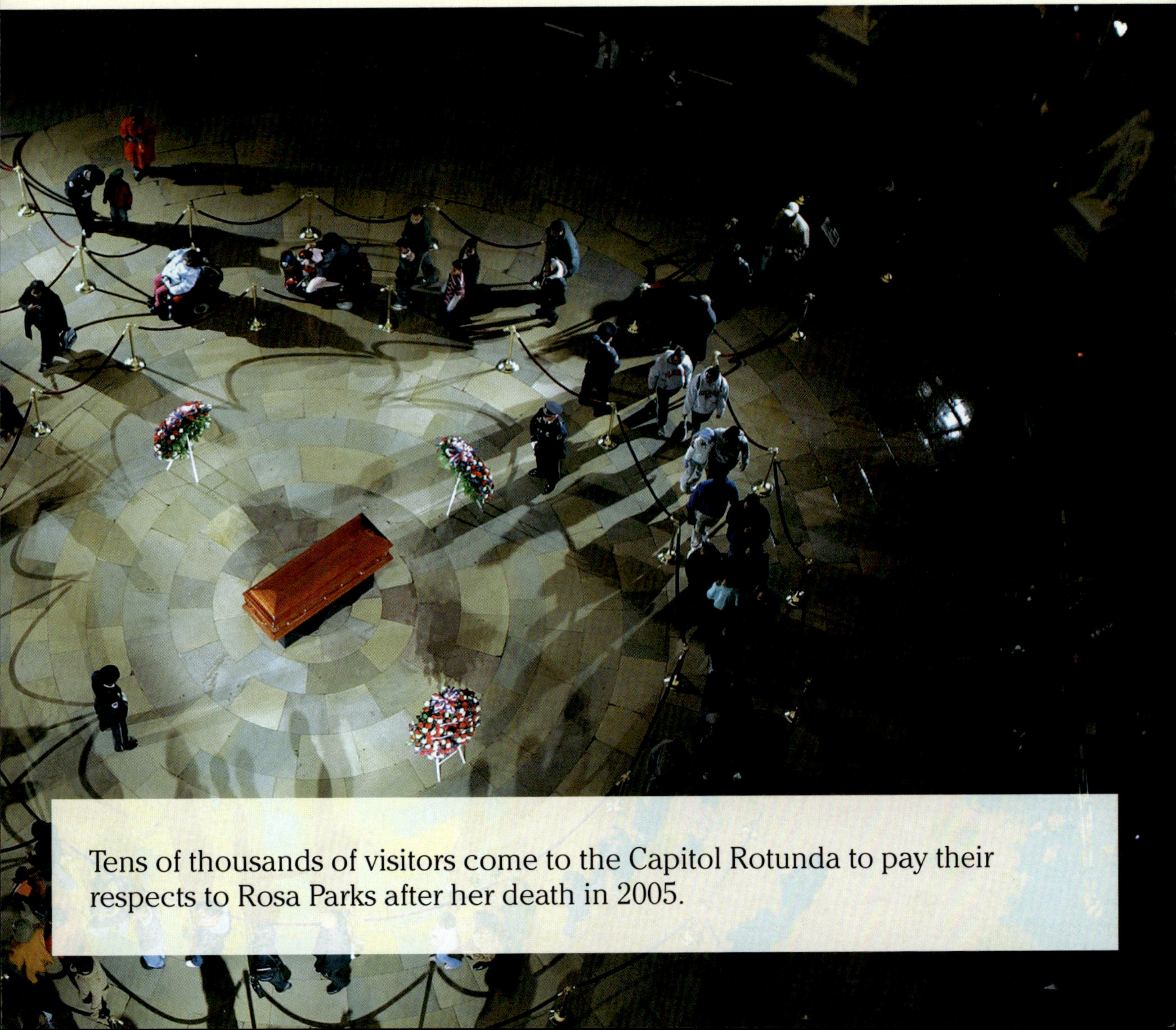

Tens of thousands of visitors come to the Capitol Rotunda to pay their respects to Rosa Parks after her death in 2005.

Still Marching

Racism didn't end with the repeal of bus segregation or the passing of the Civil Rights Act. It wasn't over when Parks died in 2005, and it's not over now. Though tremendous progress has been made, African Americans, as well as religious and ethnic minorities, immigrants, LGBTQ+ people, and the poor still struggle to make sure their constitutional rights are respected.

When Parks was an old woman—and she surely deserved a rest after her years of hard work and service—she said there were times when she hardly had the strength to "get up and go" when some cause or other needed her support. But when she did, she was rewarded by the reactions of young people. And it is, in large part, those young people, following Rosa Parks's courageous example, who are still speaking up, still marching, and still holding the nation accountable to its promise of freedom and justice for all.

The memory and spirit of Rosa Parks continues to inspire a new generation to demand economic and social justice for everyone, everywhere.

GLOSSARY

amendment A change to a legal document; specifically, an article added to the US Constitution.

apartheid An official policy of racial discrimination in South Africa from 1948 to 1994.

boycott A refusal to conduct business with or buy products from a business or organization in order to express disapproval or to attempt to change policy.

Capitol Rotunda The circular room located below the dome of the US Capitol; often considered the symbolic heart of the Capitol and used for important ceremonial events.

deference Respect and submission given to people because of their status, rank, or positions of power.

derogatory Critical, insulting, or disrespectful (typically said of comments or remarks).

ethnic Relating to a group of people, within a larger population, that is categorized by cultural characteristics, such as race, religion, language, or nation of origin.

etiquette Manners, the rules of polite or acceptable behavior in a society or group.

executive order A legally binding rule made by the president of the United States and applied to the executive branch of the government.

labor leader A person who helps workers organize, such as in trade unions, to ensure fair employment practices.

overseer A person who supervised slaves.

registrar A public official who is in charge of compiling and maintaining public records—for example, lists of registered voters.

revenue Income of a company, government, or organization.

segregation The act or policy of separating groups of people according to race.

self-esteem Self-respect or confidence in one's abilities or intrinsic value.

unconstitutional Something, such as a law, that is not in keeping with the dictates set forth by the US Constitution.

FOR MORE INFORMATION

American Civil Liberties Union (ACLU)
125 Broad Street, 18th Floor
New York, NY 10001
(212) 549-2500
Email: membership@aclu.org
Website: https://www.aclu.org
Facebook: @aclu.nationwide
Twitter: @aclu
The ACLU is an organization that works to defend and protect the individual rights and liberties that are guaranteed by the Constitution of the United States.

Birmingham Civil Rights Institute
520 Sixteenth Street North
Birmingham, AL 35203
(205) 328-9696
Email: Bcri@bcri.org
Website: http://www.bcri.org/index.html
The Birmingham Civil Rights Institute is a center and museum dedicated to enlightening each generation about the history of civil and human rights and working to build a better future.

Brennan Center for Justice
120 Broadway
Suite 1750
New York, NY 10271
(646) 292-8310
Email: brennancenter@nyu.edu
Website: http://www.brennancenter.org
Facebook: @BCRI.ORG
Twitter: @bhamcivilrights
Instagram: @bhamcivilrights

The Brennan Center for Justice is a nonpartisan law and policy institute that works to hold the United States to its promises of democracy and equal justice for all, including efforts to protect voting rights.

Congress of Black Women of Canada
c/o Congress of Black Women of Canada—Mississauga Chapter
4983 Rathkeale Road
Missussuga, ON L5V 2B3
Canada
(See other chapters for respective contact info)
(866) 986-2292
Email: Cbwontario@gmail.com
Website: http://www.cbwc-ontario.com/?page_id=5
The Congress of Black Women of Canada is a national nonprofit committed to improving the lives of black Canadian women and their families.

Websites

Because of the changing nature of internet links, Rosen Publishing has developed an online list of websites related to the subject of this book. This site is updated regularly. Please use this link to access this list:

http://www.rosenlinks.com/CIVC/Parks

FOR FURTHER READING

Branch, Taylor. *The King Years: Historic Moments in the Civil Rights Movement*. New York, NY: Simon & Schuster, 2013.

Edmonds, Michael, ed. *Risking Everything: A Freedom Summer Reader*. Madison, WI: Wisconsin Historical Society Press, 2014.

Freedman, Russell. *Because They Marched: The People's Campaign for Voting Rights That Changed America*. New York, NY: Holiday House, 2014.

McDonough, Yona Zeldis. *Who Was Rosa Parks?* New York, NY: Grosset & Dunlap, 2010.

Parks, Rosa, and Jim Haskins. *Rosa Parks: My Story*. New York, NY: Puffin, 1992.

Quinn, Barbara, and Claudia Isler. *Understanding Your Right to Vote: Personal Freedom and Civic Duty*. New York, NY: Rosen Publishing, 2012.

Theoharis, Jeanne. *The Rebellious Life of Mrs. Rosa Parks*. Boston, MA: Beacon Press, 2014.

Whitt, Margaret Earley. *Short Stories of the Civil Rights Movement: An Anthology*. Athens, GA: University of Georgia Press, 2006.

Zinn, Howard. *SNCC: The New Abolitionists*. Chicago, IL: Haymarket Books, 2013.

BIBLIOGRAPHY

Ashby, Ruth. *Rosa Parks: Courageous Citizen*. New York, NY: Sterling, 2008.

Branch, Taylor. *The King Years: Historic Moments in the Civil Rights Movement*. New York, NY: Simon & Schuster, 2013.

Brinkley, Douglas. *Rosa Parks: A Life*. New York, NY: Penguin, 2000.

Darling, Dallas. "Missing the Mark with Rosa Parks and Black History Month." Truthout.org, March 4, 2014. http://www.truth-out.org/speakout/item/14922-missing-the-mark-with-rosa-parks-and-black-history-month.

King, Martin Luther, Jr. *The Radical King*. Edited by Cornel West. Boston, MA: Beacon Press, 2015.

King, Martin Luther, Jr. *Stride Toward Freedom: The Montgomery Story.* Boston, MA: Beacon Press, 2010.

Kohl, Herbert. *She Would Not Be Moved: How We Tell the Story of Rosa Parks and the Montgomery Bus Boycott*. New York, NY: New Press, 2005.

Parks, Rosa, and Jim Haskins. *Rosa Parks: My Story*. New York, NY: Puffin, 1992.

Theoharis, Jeanne. *The Rebellious Life of Mrs. Rosa Parks*. Boston, MA: Beacon Press, 2014.

INDEX

About the Author

Avery Elizabeth Hurt lives in Birmingham, Alabama, the site of much of the history of the civil rights movement. As a child, she lived in several cities around the South and witnessed many instances of racial injustice. However, she is happy to report that the South is now a far better place than it was in Rosa Parks's day. Strolling the streets of her hometown of Birmingham gives her faith that the world can become a better place if we just keep working for it.

Photo Credits

Cover William Philpott/Hulton Archive/Getty Images; cover (background), pp. 14–15, 30–31, 32–33 Don Cravens/The LIFE Images Collection/Getty Images; pp. 5, 8–9, 18–19 Bettmann/Getty Images; pp. 6–7 Science & Society Picture Library/SSPL/Getty Images; pp. 10–11 Keystone/Hulton Archive/Getty Images; p. 12 Chicago History Museum/Archive Photos/Getty Images; p. 17 Photo 12/Universal Images Group/Getty Images; p. 21 Rex Hardy Jr./The LIFE Picture Collection/Getty Images; p. 23 The Washington Post/Getty Images; p. 25 MPI/Stringer/Archive Photos/Getty Images; p. 27 Universal Images Group/Getty Images; p. 29 New York Times Co./Archive Photos/Getty Images; pp. 35, 40–41 © AP Images; p. 37 Jeff Kowalsky/AFP/Getty Images; pp. 38–39 Joe Raedle/Getty Images; cover and interior pages designs (stars) f-64 Photo Office/amandaimagesRF /Thinkstock, (radial) ISO100/Shutterstock.com.

Design: Brian Garvey; Layout: Ellina Litmanovich;
Editor and Photo Researcher: Heather Moore Niver